topps®
MATCH ATTAX
2021

WELCOME!

Get ready for loads of football-tastic facts and fun inside this annual. Packed with stats, puzzles and games to play, you'll also find the biggest footballing legends in the world inside.

CLUB GUIDES

From Liverpool FC and Tottenham Hotspur FC to Paris Saint-Germain and Barcelona FC, check out all the top teams in Europe plus their goal-getting players.

PLAY TIME

Play like a pro and turn to page 50 for some tips and tricks to help you become a Match Attax master.

FOOTBALL HEROES

Turn to page 32 for some world-class players and page 46 for some of the highest scorers.

PLAYER MATCH

Turn to page 38 and take the quiz to work out which kind of goal scorer you are. Ready, aim, SHOOT!

GREAT GOALS

Check out page 54 for some
of the world's greatest goals... ever!

AWESOME ACTIVITIES

From word puzzles to spot-the-ball
and match-up games, put your
skills to the test with all the cool
activities inside.

ANSWERS

You can find all the
answers for the puzzles
at the back of the book.

MY AWESOME ANNUAL

Here's your chance to show you're a footy expert by picking your favourite players and teams! You can also scribble your sickest skills, reveal your footy dreams and your fave goal ever.

MY NAME: .... AGE: ....

CITY/TOWN: ....

MY SKILLS ....

POSITION: ....

TEAM I PLAY FOR: ....

MY BEST SKILL: ....

MY BEST MOMENT THIS YEAR: ....

....

....

FAVE THREE TEAMS:

1 ....

2 ....

3 ....

....

Look – this is how planes fly. Zoom, zoom!

6

FAVE UK PLAYER: ....

FAVE WORLDWIDE PLAYER: ....

....

FAVE ALL-TIME PLAYER: ....

....

BEST GOAL SEEN THIS YEAR: ....

....

FOOTY DREAMS FOR THE FUTURE:

I WANT ....

....

....

....

....

ON THE MAP!

Check out the biggest leagues and the greatest clubs from all around Europe!

A geography lesson? Get in!

Double homework for me please, teacher!

LA LIGA SPAIN

TEAMS: 20
STARTED: 1929

One of the most exciting leagues in the world! Barcelona and Real Madrid are the biggest clubs, with Atletico Madrid, Sevilla, Valencia and Villarreal also battling for glory.

PRIMEIRA LIGA PORTUGAL

TEAMS: 18
STARTED: 1934

Watch out for the top trio of Porto, Benfica and Sporting Lisbon scrapping it out for Portugal's Primeira Liga trophy! These three clubs have won every title since 2001, when Boavista were champions.

Bayern Munich won the European Cup three times in a row between 1974 and 1976

LIGUE 1 FRANCE

TEAMS: 20
STARTED: 1932

In recent years, France's Ligue 1 has been transformed into an epic league to watch. Paris Saint-Germain, Monaco, Marseille and Lyon are the big clubs chasing the title!

EREDIVISIE NETHERLANDS

TEAMS: 18
STARTED: 1956

In their orange kit, the Netherlands national team is well-known around the world. The Eredivisie league is also packed with top talent and teams like Ajax, PSV Eindhoven and Feyenoord.

BUNDESLIGA GERMANY

TEAMS: 18
STARTED: 1963

Bayern Munich, Borussia Dortmund and FC Schalke are just some of Germany's mega clubs. Stars like Robert Lewandowski and Timo Werner bash in great goals every week!

SERIE A ITALY

TEAMS: 20
STARTED: 1898

Famous clubs like Juventus, AC Milan and Inter Milan bring glitz, glamour and goals to Italy's top league! Some of the world's most amazing players have starred in Serie A.

MORE EPIC LEAGUES: Jupiler Pro League **(BELGIUM)** • Premier League **(RUSSIA)** • Primera Division **(ARGENTINA)** • Superleague **(GREECE)** • Bundesliga **(AUSTRIA)** • Super Lig **(TURKEY)** • MLS **(USA & CANADA)** • Brasileirao **(BRAZIL)**

ALL ABOUT

TOTTENHAM HOTSPUR

Here's the lowdown on this top London club's stats and stars, plus the footy facts you need to know!

TACTICS TALK

Manager José Mourinho has turned Tottenham Hotspur into one of the fiercest teams in Europe. With Harry Kane up front, the team usually sets up in a 4-2-3-1 formation. Two holding midfielders play behind forwards Son and Alli, with Aurier and Davies working hard in defence at the back.

STAR TO WATCH

LUCAS MOURA

The winger moved to Tottenham Hotspur after a £25 million switch from PSG. The exciting Brazilian took time to settle at the club, but he's ready to show the fans what a devastating mix of pace and power he has. His right foot can light up Spurs' attacks!

TEAM HERO GLENN HODDLE

One of the most stylish midfielders Spurs have ever produced, Glenn Hoddle starred for the club between 1975 and 1987. He made 377 league appearances, scored 88 goals and won the FA Cup and UEFA Cup. Hoddle also managed England from 1996 to 1999 and Spurs from 2001 to 2003.

3 SICK STARS

HEUNG-MIN SON With his right foot, left foot or head, Son scores all sorts of crucial goals for Tottenham. He links up superbly with Kane.

JAN VERTONGHEN The experienced centre-back keeps Spurs' backline strong and uses his positional sense to cut out danger.

DELE ALLI Using his slick skills, speed, passing and quality shooting, Alli always does the business from his attacking midfield spot.

DID YOU KNOW?

Harry Kane
went to the
same school as
David Beckham
– but not at the
same time!

☆STAR PLAYER

HARRY KANE

POSITION: Striker
BORN: UK, 1993

Goals, goals, goals! That's the best way
to describe Harry Kane. The England
ace has all the skills – power, vision,
accuracy, heading and a natural goal instinct.

ALL ABOUT

MANCHESTER CITY

One of the richest clubs in the world, Manchester City boasts some of the world's top players, who are always seeking to top the footy leagues at home and away.

TACTICS TALK

Manager Pep Guardiola unleashes players like Kevin De Bruyne, Leroy Sane and Raheem Sterling in lightning-quick attacks. Defenders Kyle Walker and Bejamin Mendy race down the wings to cross and set up strikers Sergio Aguero and Gabriel Jesus.

TEAM HERO

GEORGI KINKLADZE

The tricky midfielder was a sensational Manchester City hero between 1995 and 1998. He scored wonder goals and dribbled past defenders as if they were statues. Kinkladze even turned down Barcelona to stay at the club!

STAR TO WATCH

PHIL FODEN

The 18-year-old won the Under-17 World Cup with England in 2017. An exciting midfielder who loves to score and create goals – this left-footed ace always rips it up.

3 SICK STARS

DAVID SILVA The little Spaniard bosses Manchester City's midfield, helping to set up goals.

EDERSON The keeper cost a mega £35 million in 2017, but he was worth every penny.

RAHEEM STERLING Playing on the right, left or in the middle, the England forward can always be counted on.

DID YOU KNOW?

This clever midfielder can speak fluent Dutch, French and English.

⭐ STAR PLAYER

KEVIN DE BRUYNE
POSITION: Midfielder
BORN: BELGIUM, 1991

Dazzling De Bruyne is on top form. The brilliant Belgium attacker floats between midfield and attack, whipping laser-guided passes to Aguero and Jesus and delivering perfect free-kicks and corners.

13

WHO SCORED?

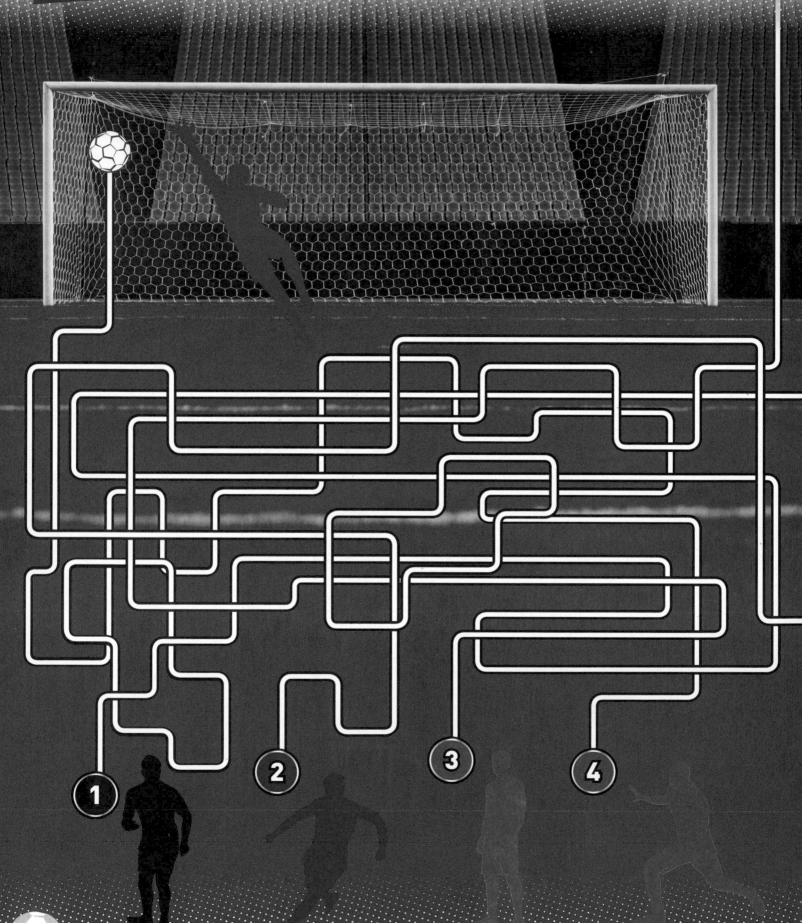

USE YOUR HEAD!

Prove you're champion quality by solving every clue!

Solve each clue in this brain-busting crossword to take home some silverware.

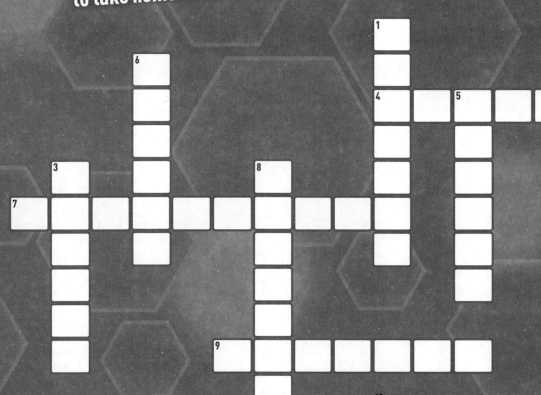

DOWN

1 Another word for a win. (7)

2 To move the ball up the pitch close to your body. (7)

3 To strike the ball before it touches the ground. (6)

5 The last pass before a goal is scored. (6)

6 When you steal the ball from an opponent. (6)

8 The person in charge of a football match. (7)

ACROSS

4 The team that wins the league will be the _____. (9)

7 The only person that can handle the ball on the pitch. (10)

9 This is awarded if a foul is committed in the 18-yard box. (7)

ALL ABOUT

LIVERPOOL FC

Jurgen Klopp's entertaining and talented team always plays to the crowd to produce exciting games and thrilling results.

TACTICS TALK

With an epic attacking trio of Mohamed Salah, Roberto Firmino and Sadio Mane, manager Klopp usually starts with a 4-3-3 set up, with Virgil Van Dijk controlling the defence and captain Jordan Henderson bossing central midfield.

3 SICK STARS

ROBERTO FIRMINO The slick-skilled Brazilian has become a top-class No.9 for The Reds with his pace and penalty box skills.

ALEX OXLADE-CHAMBERLAIN Liverpool paid £35 million for the versatile midfielder. He's worth every penny with his non-stop running and goal threat.

JORDAN HENDERSON He skippers the team very well, making vital tackles and precise passes to release Liverpool's lightning-quick attackers.

STAR TO WATCH

TRENT ALEXANDER-ARNOLD

The young defender was born in Liverpool and is a first-team regular for The Reds, the team he supported as a boy. Alexander-Arnold also plays for England and is one of the best full-backs in the world on his current form.

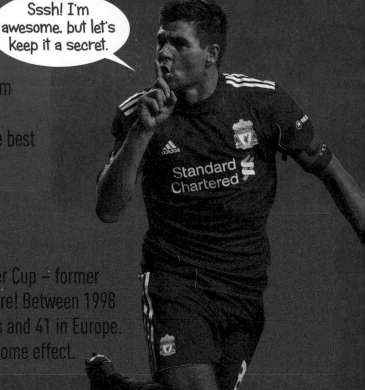

Sssh! I'm awesome, but let's keep it a secret.

TEAM HERO STEVEN GERRARD

UEFA Champions League, FA Cup, League Cup, UEFA Super Cup – former Liverpool FC captain Steven Gerrard has bags of silverware! Between 1998 and 2015, the central midfielder scored 120 league goals and 41 in Europe. Stevie G mixed power, vision and quality passing to awesome effect.

MOHAMED SALAH

DID YOU KNOW?

Virgil Van Dijk joined The Reds for £75 million in 2018, which was a world record for a defender.

☆ STAR PLAYER

MOHAMED SALAH

POSITION: Forward

BORN: Egypt, 1992

Wow! What skills Mohamed Salah brings to Liverpool FC! After joining in summer 2017, the skillful Egyptian's left-foot defeated defenders and combined with slick skills and turbo speed, it's no surprise that Salah is one the most feared goal scorers.

17

CHELSEA

This top London team have a trophy cabinet full of silverware and a squad that's packed with world-class heroes.

TACTICS TALK

Fank Lampard, Chelsea's manager approaches the games with an attacking mentality. His preference for a passing style makes for exciting games and he works to utilise the skills of three of his most valuable players, Kante, Abraham and Mount.

3 SICK STARS

KEPA ARRIZABALAGA Controls his goal with incredible saves and reflexes, making him a vital part of the team.

TAMMY ABRAHAM This young striker is a beast in the box and a clinical goal scorer.

WILLIAN The busy Brazilian is always full of energy, skill and pace. He strikes a sweet free-kick with his right boot, too!

TEAM HERO

FRANK LAMPARD

Goal scoring midfielder Lampard played for The Blues from 2001 to 2014. In that time he clocked up 648 games, bagged a record 211 goals and secured 11 major honours. Lamps is also the highest-scoring midfielder in UK history with 177 goals.

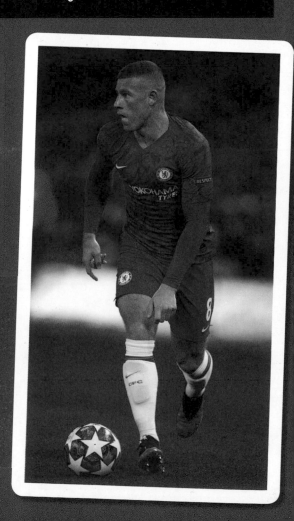

STAR TO WATCH

ROSS BARKLEY

Injury meant the England midfielder hardly played for Chelsea at first, after joining from Everton. When he's fully fit, the £15 million man loves to boss the pitch and break forward to support attacks. Big things are expected of this exciting player!

MARCOS ALONSO

MARCOS ALONSO

POSITION: Defender

BORN: SPAIN, 1990

Alonso was born in Madrid and is the son and grandson of former Spain internationals. Currently he has made the starting line up for 5 games in the 2019/20 UEFA Champions League with an 80% tackle success rate.

DID YOU KNOW?

Olivier Giroud is an awesome header of the ball - with many of his most memorable goals scored with his head.

MATCH REPORT

Puzzle over these questions from a crazy cup tie (we made up the result). How well will you score?

1 If kick-off is at 3pm and the first half lasts 45 minutes, draw the hands on the clock to show when half-time is.

2 Sterling scores a goal at 3:19. How many minutes is this into the game?

ANSWER:

3 Firmino equalises 4 minutes before half-time. In which minute did he score?

ANSWER:

4 Half-time lasts 15 minutes. When will it be time to kick off again?

ANSWER:

5 Stones receives a yellow card 11 minutes after half-time. How many minutes have been played altogether?

ANSWER:

6 Salah gets injured 2 minutes later. How many minutes have been played now?

ANSWER:

7 Mane comes on as a sub after 76 minutes. How many minutes will he play for if the game is won in 90 minutes?

ANSWER:

8 Lallana is shown a red card with just two minutes left on the clock. In which minute was he sent off?

ANSWER:

9 The match goes to extra-time, with 30 minutes added on. How many minutes will have been played altogether?

ANSWER:

10 It's a penalty shootout! Manchester City win 4–2 on penalties. How many penalties found the back of the net?

ANSWER:

GO FOR GOAL!

Help this attacking player dribble through the maze, dodging defenders along the way to reach the goal.

START

 GOAL

ALL ABOUT

BARCELONA

Superstar Spanish club Barcelona is packed with talent, trophies and top new signings every year! Discover more about Barca's amazing story and success...

BRILL BARCA!

You could fill a book with the victories, epic players and fantastic history of Barcelona! This skilful Spanish team have been the most eye-catching club this century and had some of the best players on the planet. Footy legends like Andres Iniesta, Gerard Pique and Lionel Messi came through the club's famous youth system and heroes such as Luis Suarez and Ousmane Dembele arrived in mega transfers.

STARS TO WATCH...

LUIS SUAREZ	OUSMANE DEMBELE	GERARD PIQUE
STRIKER	WINGER	DEFENDER
Powerful shots & top tricks	Dribble & speed king	Strong & clever on the ball

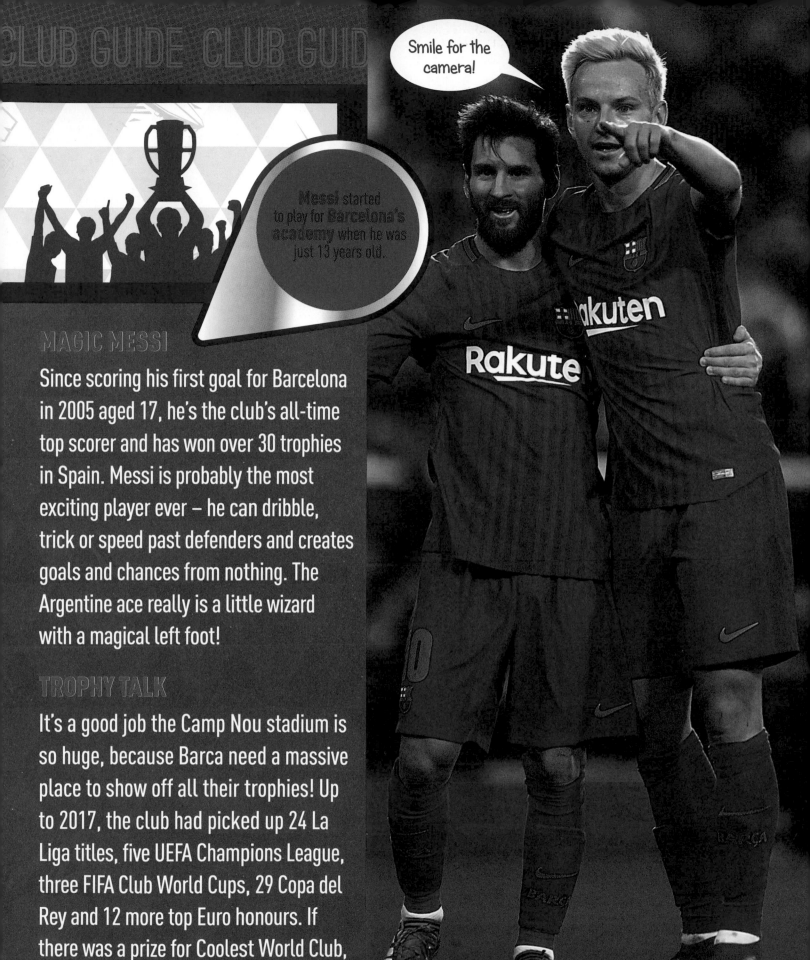

Smile for the camera!

Messi started to play for Barcelona's academy when he was just 13 years old.

MAGIC MESSI

Since scoring his first goal for Barcelona in 2005 aged 17, he's the club's all-time top scorer and has won over 30 trophies in Spain. Messi is probably the most exciting player ever – he can dribble, trick or speed past defenders and creates goals and chances from nothing. The Argentine ace really is a little wizard with a magical left foot!

TROPHY TALK

It's a good job the Camp Nou stadium is so huge, because Barca need a massive place to show off all their trophies! Up to 2017, the club had picked up 24 La Liga titles, five UEFA Champions League, three FIFA Club World Cups, 29 Copa del Rey and 12 more top Euro honours. If there was a prize for Coolest World Club, they'd walk off with that one too!

CAPTAIN: Lionel Messi **NEW SIGNING:** Matheus Fernandes **ATTACKING MIDFIELDER:** Alex Collado

WORLD SUPERSTARS

★ ★ ★ ★ ★

From Pele to Cruyff and Maradona to Maldini, discover why this bunch of brilliant world superstars are the biggest heroes, past and present.

> Help! This thing is well heavy!

DIEGO MARADONA

MAIN CLUBS: Boca Juniors, Napoli, Barcelona
POSITION: STRIKER
COUNTRY: Argentina
- Lead Napoli to Serie A title in 1987 and 1990
- Superstar of the 1986 World Cup
- Strength, skills and epic dribbling

EUSEBIO

MAIN CLUB: Benfica
POSITION: Striker
COUNTRY: Portugal
- Incredible record of 727 goals in 715 Benfica games
- Golden Boot winner at 1966 World Cup
- Deadly hitman with 11 titles in Portugal

RONALDINHO

MAIN CLUBS: AC Milan, Barcelona, PSG
POSITION: Forward
COUNTRY: Brazil
- Super skilful winger or striker
- La Liga, Serie A and UEFA Champions League winner
- World Cup hero with Brazil in 2002

ALFREDO DI STEFANO

MAIN CLUB: Real Madrid
POSITION: Striker
COUNTRY: Spain and Argentina

- Five European Cup victories
- Superstar striker in 1950s and '60s
- Powerful, with laser-like shooting

PELE

MAIN CLUB: Santos
POSITION: Striker
COUNTRY: Brazil

- Won World Cup in 1958, 1962 and 1970
- Deadly accurate in front of goal
- Career record of 1,281 goals

GEORGE BEST

MAIN CLUB: Manchester United
POSITION: Forward
COUNTRY: Northern Ireland

- Red Devils megastar in 1960s and '70s
- Deadly dribbling, speed, tricks and shooting
- 179 goals in 470 Manchester United games

PAOLO MALDINI

CLUB: AC Milan
POSITION: Defender
COUNTRY: Italy

- Played 902 games and won 26 trophies with Milan
- Cool on the ball, tough, with a sweet left foot
- Five times UEFA Champions League winner

I've got more medals than you've had hot dinners!

25

WORLD SUPERSTARS ★ ★ ★ ★ ★

FRANZ BECKENBAUER

MAIN CLUB: Bayern Munich
POSITION: Defender
COUNTRY: Germany
- Stylish centre-back and sweeper
- Three European Cups and five Bundesligas
- World Cup winner as player and coach

RONALDO

MAIN CLUBS: Real Madrid, Inter Milan and Barcelona
POSITION: Striker
COUNTRY: Brazil
- World Cup star in 1998, 2002, 2006
- Amazing speed, tricks and shooting
- Two La Liga titles with Real Madrid

MICHEL PLATINI

MAIN CLUBS: Juventus, St-Etienne
POSITION: Forward
COUNTRY: France
- Serie A and European Cup winner
- Amazing goalscorer and leader
- Speed, skills and intelligence

GERD MULLER

MAIN CLUB: Bayern Munich
POSITION: Striker
COUNTRY: Germany
- Club record 533 goals for Bayern
- Five Bundesliga and three European Cup titles
- World Cup winner in 1974

MIROSLAV KLOSE

MAIN CLUBS: Lazio, Bayern Munich, Werder Bremen
POSITION: Striker
COUNTRY: Germany

- Germany legend with 16 World Cup finals goals
- Record 71 strikes in 137 international games
- Awesome header of the ball

ROBERTO BAGGIO

MAIN CLUBS: AC Milan, Juventus, Fiorentina
POSITION: Forward
COUNTRY: Italy

- Serie A winner with Juventus and Milan
- Amazing dribbling and free-kicks
- Starred at 1990, 1994 and 1998 World Cup

JOHAN CRUYFF

MAIN CLUBS: Ajax, Barcelona
POSITION: Forward
COUNTRY: Netherlands

- Stylish, skilful and great vision
- Three European Player of the Year awards
- European Cup winner as player and coach

You can call me Zizou!

Zidane starred for France at the 2006, 2002 and 1998 World Cup.

ZINEDINE ZIDANE

MAIN CLUBS: Real Madrid, Juventus
POSITION: Midfielder
COUNTRY: France

- Three World Player of the Year trophies
- World Cup and Champions League winner
- Magical skills, control, power and passing

ALL ABOUT

BAYERN MUNICH

German clubs don't come any bigger than the brilliant Bayern Munich! The Bundesliga greats are a worldwide superpower with stacks of success.

PLAYER POWER

With the likes of Thomas Muller, Joshua Kimmich and Thiago Alcantara Bayern's squad is one of the best in Europe. Plus, Bayern have the goalscoring skills of Robert Lewandowski – one of the most dangerous strikers on the planet!

GERMAN GIANTS

Thanks to a record 28 German titles between 1932 and 2019, Bayern Munich's trophy cabinet is absolutely stuffed! The last time they finished outside of the top two was way back in 2007 and they now have seven league championships in a row. With over 30 German cups and five UEFA Champions Leagues up to 2013, it's a huge shock if Bayern don't win at least one trophy every season.

STARS TO WATCH...

THOMAS MULLER
FORWARD
Goalscorer & creator

KINGSLEY COMAN
WINGER
Speedy & skilful

MANUEL NEUER
GOALKEEPER
Awesome saves & kicking

Robert Lewandowski first wore the Bayern No.9 in 2014 after moving from Bundesliga rivals Borussia Dortmund.

In 2015, Bayern's No.9 scored a record five Bundesliga goals in just nine minutes against Wolfsburg.

Lewandowski's a goal creator too, clocking up 94 assists in 397 appearances for club and country.

Robert needed just 136 games to crack in his 100th Bayern Munich goal in all competitions.

He helped Poland reach the 2018 World Cup by netting a European record of 16 goals in qualifying.

Lewandowski moved into the top ten all-time UEFA Champions League goal scorers in 2018 with his 45th strike in 67 games.

The Poland captain has been voted his country's Player of the Year seven times in a row!

In 250 Bundesliga games, Robert smashed an unbelievable 171 goals!

In 2013 he blasted four goals in a UEFA Champions League semi-final for Borussia Dortmund against Real Madrid.

CAPTAIN: Manuel Neuer **TOP SCORER:** Gerd Muller (533) **YOUNG STAR:** Christian Fruchtl

GAME TIME!

Find a friend and challenge them to this fun game.

1 Take it in turns to draw a vertical or horizontal line between each dot on the board below.

2 Each time you complete a box, mark your initials inside it.

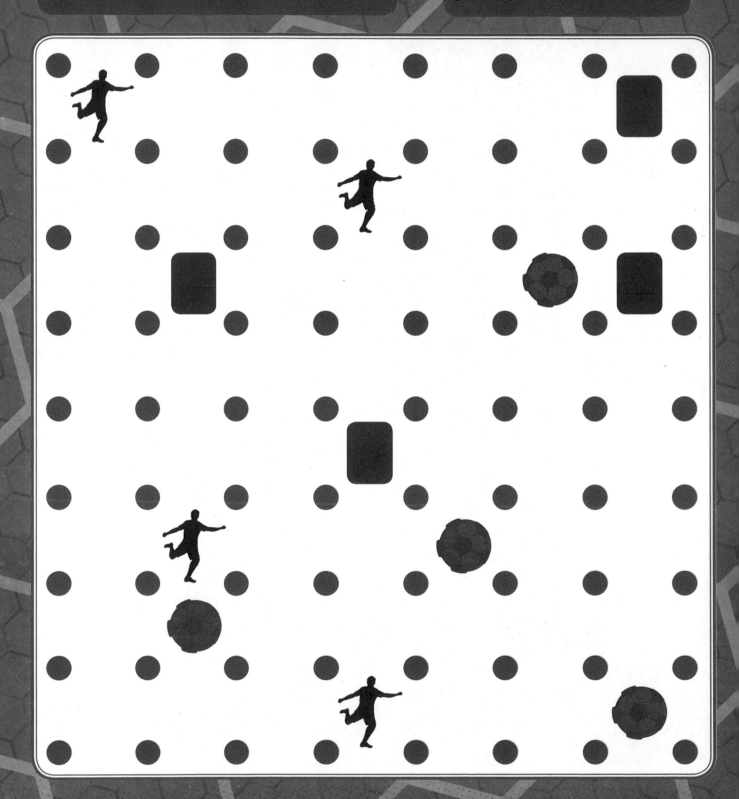

30

3 An empty box is worth 1 point, a football box is worth 2 points, a striker box is worth 3 points and a red card box is worth -1 point.

4 When all the dots have been joined up, add up your scores. The player with the most points, wins. Don't worry if you lose, just play again on the board below.

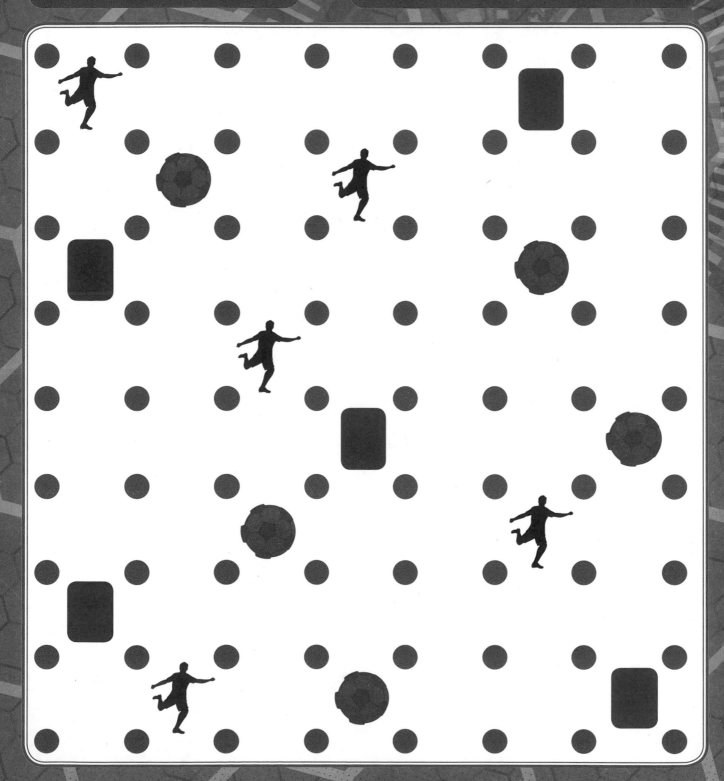

BATTLE OF THE BIG GUNS!

Ronaldo, Messi and Neymar have been voted the three best players on the planet. Check out their goals, stats and trophy hauls!

CRISTIANO RONALDO

Club: Juventus

Position: Left Winger

Full name: Cristiano Ronaldo dos Santos Aveiro

Nickname: Ronnie, CR7

Date of Birth: 5 February, 1985

Place of Birth: Funchal, Madeira, Portugal

Height: 1.87 m **Weight:** 84 kg

Left or Right Footed: Both

International Team: Portugal

Game appearances:	836
Goals:	626
Assists:	219
Yellow cards:	99
Red cards:	7
UEFA Champions League Winner :	7

This is my totally serious about scoring face.

Ronaldo is head and shoulders above the rest of the world when it comes to UEFA Champions League goals – by April 2018, he'd scored 117 times in the competition!

NEYMAR JR

Club: Paris Saint-Germain

Position: Forward

Full name: Neymar da Silva Santos Júnior

Nicknames: 'O Joia' (The gem), NJR

Date of Birth: 5 February, 1992

Place of Birth: São Paulo, Brazil

Height: 1.75 m **Weight:** 68 kg

Left or Right Footed: Both

International Team: Brazil

Game appearances:	400
Goals:	244
Assists:	151
Yellow cards:	105
Red cards:	2
UEFA Champions League Winner :	1

During his time at Barcelona, Messi has won 30 major honours. Let's hope his trophy cabinet is big enough!

LIONEL MESSI

Club: Barcelona

Position: Forward

Full name: Lionel Andrés Messi Cuccittini

Nicknames: 'La Pulga' (The Flea)

Date of Birth: 24 June, 1987

Place of Birth: Rosario, Argentina

Height: 1.70 m **Weight:** 72 kg

Left or Right Footed: Left

International Team: Argentina

Game appearances:	718
Goals:	627
Assists:	261
Yellow cards:	75
Red cards:	0
UEFA Champions League Winner :	4

Neymar's massive £198-million move from Barcelona to Paris Saint-Germain smashed the world-record fee for a transfer.

PUZZLE IT OUT

Can you work out the sums below using the answers already given?

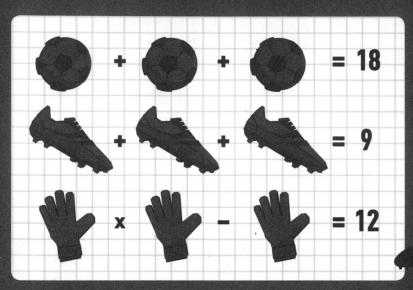 + + = 18

 + + = 9

 x − = 12

1   +  +  =

2   x  − 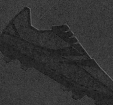 =

3    x  + 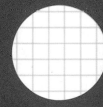 =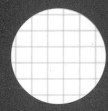

4   −  +  =

34

SPOT THE BALL

Can you count up all the large, medium and small balls in the puzzle below?

I counted _____ large balls.

I counted _____ medium balls.

I counted _____ small balls.

ANSWERS AT BACK OF BOOK.

35

JUVENTUS

Juventus boss Serie A! The Italian masters have fantastic players, bags of trophies and amazing fans. Take a close look at the awesome Italians...

PLAYER POWER

Juventus' squad is boosted by many of Serie A's top stars. After selling Paul Pogba to Manchester United in 2016, they bought striker Gonzalo Higuain for a huge £75 million. Higuan scored 24 league goals in his first season and he's supported in attack by Paulo Dybala and Cristiano Ronaldo. Gianluigi Buffon has been a legendary keeper since joining in 2001 and Andrea Barzagli and Giorgio Chiellini proved a tough centre-back duo.

TROPHY TALK

In 2019, Juventus picked up a record 35th Italian top-flight championship. It was also the first time any club had won eight Serie A titles in a row! The Old Lady are European heavyweights with two UEFA Champions League crowns, but they have lost Europe's biggest final seven times, including 2017 and 2015. Up to 2019, Juve also had 13 wins Coppa Italia and eight Italian Super Cup trophies. There's plenty of silverware on show!

STARS TO WATCH...

MIRALEM PJANIC
MIDFIELDER
Cool head bosses games

JUAN CUADRADO
WINGER
Speed & slick right foot

SAMI KHEDIRA
MIDFIELDER
Brings goals & epic passing

GONZALO HIGUAIN
STRIKER
Pure goal machine

Forward Paulo Dybala first wore No.10 for Juventus in August 2017. He had No.21 when he joined from Palermo in 2015.

He scored 45 Serie A goals in his first 86 games for Juve.

Before Juventus, the attacker spent three seasons in Serie A with Palermo.

Dybala also plays for Argentina and made his first international appearance in 2015.

The Juventus No.10 is a speedy forward and can reach speeds of 29 km per hour on the pitch!

His first UEFA Champions League goal was against Bayern Munich in 2016.

He was born in November 1993.

In 2017-18, Dybala scored 12 of his first 15 Serie A goals with his left foot.

He's a free-kick king who loves to whip the ball over the wall!

His favourite foot is his left.

CAPTAIN: Giorgio Chiellini **BIG BUY:** Gonzalo Higuain (£75M in 2016) **YOUNG STAR:** Rodrigo Bentancur

WHICH GOALSCORER ARE YOU?

START

Does your game use **speed and vision**, or are you a **powerful player** who battles defenders?

SPEED

POWER

Do you usually take **penalties** for your team?

NO

YES

Can you score with **both** your right and left feet?

YES

YES

Do you often try to score from **free-kicks**?

YES

NO

NO

YES

Are you famous for a **leaping goal celebration**?

Would you prefer to play in a red kit or a blue kit?

RED

BLUE

NO

NO

Have you scored lots of **headed goals** in your league?

YES

YOU'RE
MO SALAH
The Liverpool FC goal machine is super speedy, lets rip with his lethal left foot and looks awesome in red!

YOU'RE
EDEN HAZARD
Hazard mixes his pace and skills on the pitch and can score spectacular goals from penalties, free-kicks and outside the box!

YOU'RE
CRISTIANO RONALDO
The Juventus striker has netted over 100 headers and constantly causes headaches for defenders.

TRADING CARD GAME

Play in 3 exciting game modes!

- Show off your tactical expertise as you progress through the Match Attax leagues.
- Go head-to-head with other Match Attax collectors in our free weekly tournaments.
- Take on your friends and family with our Head-to-Head mode.

SPEED 97
TACKLE 43
POWER 73
SHOOT 94
SKILL 94
PASS 89

MBAPPÉ
FORWARD £14.0M
DEFENCE 40 ATTACK 98

SCAN THIS CODE FOR A FREE DIGITAL PACKET!

Your own Trophy Cabinet!

You Won the Tournament!
Leeds Cobras

Fill your own personal Trophy Cabinet with our exciting in-app reward system.
Earn trophies for collecting, swapping and playing within the app, including a trophy that means you have to attack with a defender!

FREE APP CODE IN EVERY PACK

DOWNLOAD AND PLAY THE APP!

ENJOY ALL THIS IN THE APP PLUS MUCH, MUCH MORE!

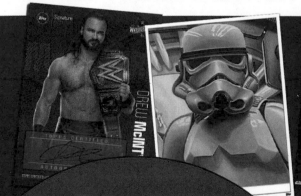

ALL ABOUT

REAL MADRID

Goals, superstars, trophies and top transfers – Real Madrid fans always have plenty to cheer about at the Bernabeu!

Marcelo Da Silva was born in 1988 in Rio de Janeiro, Brazil. He weighs 75kg and is 1.74m tall.

GAME PLAN

Zinedine Zidane has packed his team with goalscoring talent. Gareth Bale and Karim Benzema have over 250 club strikes between them and midfielders Marco Asensio, Isco, Luka Modric and Toni Kroos set up stacks of chances. Rock-hard defender Sergio Ramos also loves to hit the net!

TROPHY TALK

UEFA Champions League, La Liga, FIFA Club World Cup, UEFA Super Cup trophies... Real Madrid have lifted them all this decade! The Whites won 33 league titles between 1932 and 2017 and became the first club to win consecutive UEFA Champions League titles in 2016 and 2017. That year they won Europe's top prize for a record 12th time.

STARS TO WATCH...

JAMES RODRÍGUEZ
MIDFIELDER
Creative passer

RAPHAEL VARANE
DEFENDER
Perfect tackler

ISCO
MIDFIELDER
Trickster with ace shooting

GARETH BALE
FORWARD
Skilful left foot

CAPTAIN: Sergio Ramos **BIG BUY:** Gareth Bale (£85m in 2013) **YOUNG STAR:** Éder Militao

ATLETICO MADRID

Barcelona and Real Madrid need to watch out – Atletico Madrid are shooting for Spanish glory! It's time to reveal just how talented the team is...

GOAL GETTERS

Although Diego Simeone has turned Atletico Madrid into a very tough team to beat with powerful defenders, they also have some of the best attacking talent in Spain! Diego Costa fires in the goals in the league and Europe. Sergio Aguero, Radamel Falcao and Diego Forlan have all smashed the net for Atletico in the 21st century!

TROPHY TALK

Awesome Atletico Madrid are the third most successful club in La Liga, after Real Madrid and Barcelona. Between 1940 and 2014 they lifted ten championships and secured ten Copa del Rey wins. Legendary manager Diego Simeone is the man behind their recent success, but they lost the 2014 and 2016 UEFA Champions League finals to fierce city rivals Real Madrid.

STARS TO WATCH...

RENAN LODI
DEFENDER
Amazing heading skills

KOKE
MIDFIELDER
Bosses games with ease

SAUL NIGUEZ
MIDFIELDER
Creative & energetic

CAPTAINS: Koke is the official captain with Oblak as vice-captain and Gimenez as third captain.

43

VALENCIA FC

On the sunny east coast of Spain, Valencia FC's bright talents hope to take the club back to their European glory days!

GAME PLAN

Valencia FC is the third most supported team behind Barcelona and Real Madrid. After achieving much success with manager Marcelino, including a return to the UEFA Champions League and winning the Copa del Rey for the first time since 2008, the club is now managed by Albert Celades López, who is a former Spanish former defensive midfielder.

PLAYER POWER

The backbone of Valencia FC is Ezequiel Garay in defence, Dani Parejo and Geoffrey Kondogbia controlling midfield and Rodrigo snapping in attack. Francis Coquelin was signed from Arsenal to boost the middle of the pitch, with Goncalo Guedes and Carlos Soler defending and running down the wings. Valencia FC created a top team work-rate to take on the bigger Spanish teams!

STARS TO WATCH...

★★★☆☆

FRANCIS COQUELIN	**GABRIEL PAULISTA**	**JUAME DOMÉNECH**
MIDFIELDER	DEFENDER	GOALKEEPER
Plays anywhere in midfield	Top tackling	Strong in the box

CAPTAIN: Dani Parejo   **TOP SCORER:** Maxi Gómez   **YOUNG STAR:** Ferran Torres

BORUSSIA DORTMUND

With Bundesliga and UEFA Champions League trophies, Borussia Dortmund can flex their muscles with the best clubs in Europe! Check out their top stats and stars.

GROUND FORCE

The atmosphere at the mighty Signal Iduna Park is unlike anywhere else in Germany! It's the biggest ground in the country, with its south stand alone housing 24,454 fans, and generates a monster sound when Dortmund turn on the style and hit the net. The stadium opened in 1974 and every Bundesliga player looks forward to running out at this legendary venue.

TROPHY TALK

Borussia Dortmund have won three Bundesliga titles in the 21st century, with eight in total, plus nine major German cups up to 2017. In 1997, Dortmund were the first German club to win the UEFA Champions League.

EPIC ENGLAND STAR

Teenager Jadon Sancho surprisingly left Manchester City in 2017 to make his mark in the Bundesliga. The midfielder helped England win the Under-17 World Cup. Sancho's full of slick skills and loves to burst forward to create and score goals!

STARS TO WATCH...

JULIAN BRANDT
MIDFIELDER
Clever goalscorer

MARCO REUS
STRIKER
Ace attacking skills

ROMAN BURKI
GOALKEEPER
Last man standing

CAPTAIN: Marco Reus **TOP SCORER:** Jadon Sancho **MIDFIELD ANCHOR:** Axel Witsel

GOLDEN GREATS

Check out these stats and facts about the golden goalscorers who have picked up Europe's hottest striking prize – the Golden Shoe!

The Golden Shoe is given to the highest-scoring player in European league footy each season.

Goals scored in the big five leagues (England, Germany, France, Italy and Spain) earn two points. Each goal in smaller leagues is worth 1 or 1.5 points.

It began in 1968, with Benfica striker Eusebio taking the trophy with 42 league goals.

Portuguese master!

Thierry Henry has also racked up two Golden Shoe awards, winning in 2004 and 2005.

Lionel Messi was presented with his sixth European Golden Shoe award in 2019 after netting 36 goals in Barcelona's triumphant La Liga campaign in 2018/19.

Luis Suarez scooped the European Golden Shoe in 2014 (tied with Ronaldo) and in 2016.

I'll add this to my collection!

Cristiano Ronaldo has also racked up four Golden Shoe awards, winning in 2008, 2011, 2014 and 2015.

MATCH UP!

Can you match the footy icons into pairs?

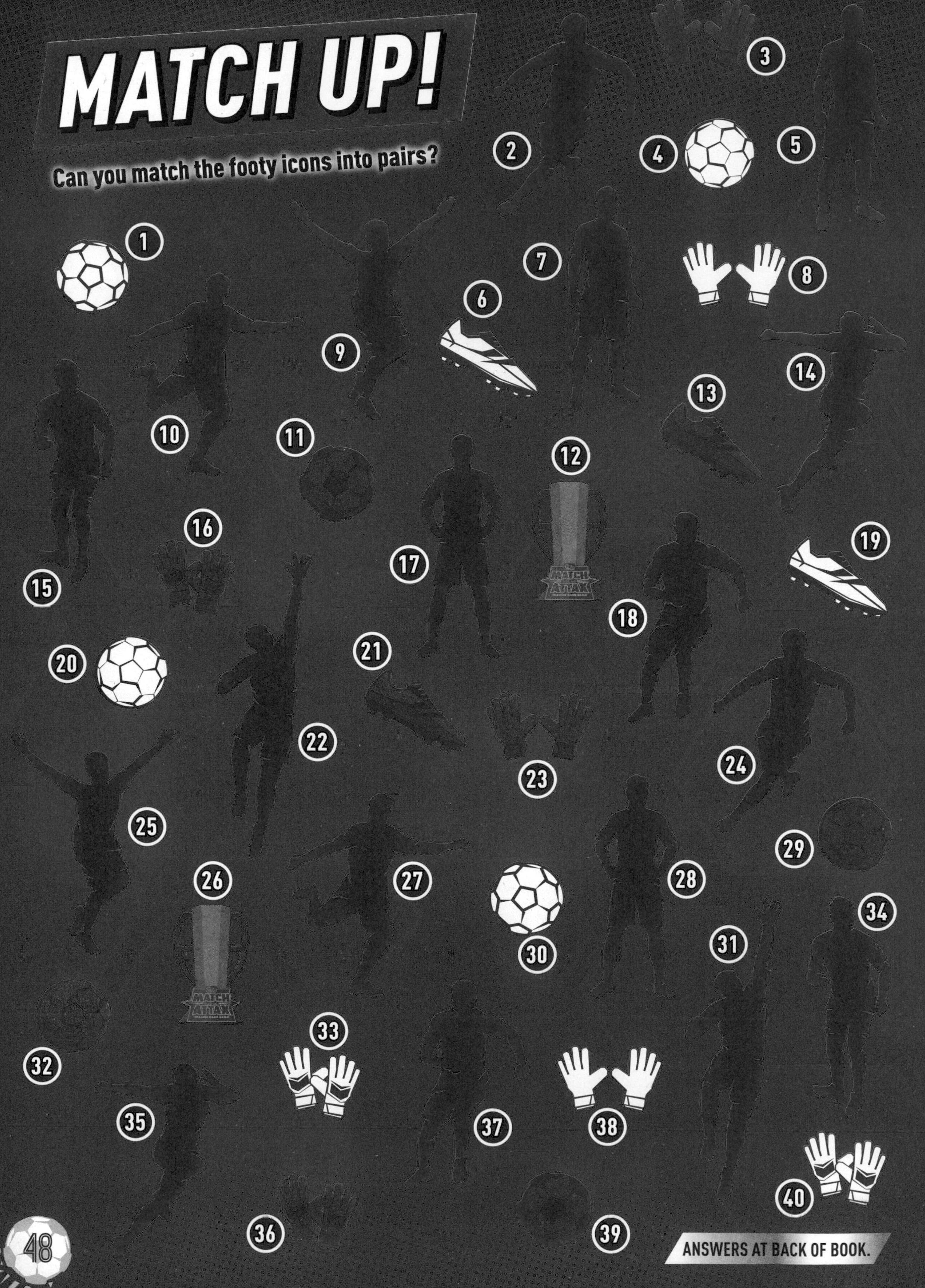

1

2

3

4

5

6

7

8

9

10

11

12

13

14

15

16

17

18

19

20

21

22

23

24

25

26

27

28

29

30

31

32

33

34

35

36

37

38

39

40

ANSWERS AT BACK OF BOOK.

48

ALL ABOUT

RB LEIPZIG

An exciting team with an amazing success story in recent years – RB Leipzig are Bundesliga giants with a big future!

RB LEIPZIG TIMELINE

2010	Oberliga champions
2011	Regionalliga fourth
2012	Regionalliga third
2013	Regionalliga champions
2014	3. Liga runners-up
2015	2. Bundesliga fifth
2016	2. Bundesliga runners-up
2017	Bundesliga runners-up
2018	Bundesliga sixth
2019	Bundesliga third

UEFA CHAMPIONS LEAGUE

Just eight years after their very first game, RB Leipzig played in the UEFA Champions League! In the 2017-18 season the club won twice and drew one game in Group G, with top deliverer Emil Forsberg scoring their first European goal. In the UEFA Europa League that season, The Bulls pulled off another shock by beating Serie A leaders Napoli. The Germans will definitely be a Euro force for years to come.

NABY KEITA

Behind RB Leipzig's sensational Bundesliga rise was power-packed central midfielder, Naby Keita. The Guinea star joined the team in 2016 and hit 15 goals and ten assists in his first 57 games. He was like Lionel Messi and N'Golo Kante all rolled into one – a skilful attacking star who won the ball in the middle of the pitch for The Bulls. Sadly for the team he was bought by Liverpool FC in 2018 and is now delighting the fans in Anfield with his onfield skills.

STARS TO WATCH...

DAYOT UPAMECANO
DEFENDER
Talented on the ball

TIMO WERNER
STRIKER
Star German goalscorer

YUSSUF POULSEN
STRIKER
Strong team player

PETER GULACSI
GOALKEEPER
Awesome shot-stopper

CAPTAIN: Willi Orban **SURPRISE SIGNING:** Ademola Lookman **STAR STRIKER:** Timo Werner

MATCH ATTAX

PLAY TO WIN!

As every football manager knows, you need strategy as well as top players to be a winner. Here are five top tips to help you collect and play like a pro. You'll soon be a Match Attax master!

I'm a hat-trick hero!

1 101 – THE ULTIMATE MATCH ATTAX CARD

Look out for the 101-rated card in packets. The 101-er is unbeatable so it's a no-brainer to get one into your line-up!

2 AWAY KITS AND HAT-TRICK HEROES!

Away Kit cards feature players in their team's alternative strip and are a must-have for your team. These cool cards could score you two goals meaning playing from home need never be a problem again. Also don't miss out on Hat-Trick Heroes, featuring players who've scored trebles throughout the season. They could score you three goals!

3 SUPER SUBS!

Each team has 11 players and 3 subs so if you want to switch things up, you'll need a good impact player coming off the bench. You can surprise an opponent and turn the game in your favour with a well-timed sub!

MATCH ATTAX APP!

How to collect, swap and play with thousands of players around the world on the Match Attax App:

STEP 1. Search Match Attax on your App store.

STEP 2. Download the Match Attax App.

STEP 3. Scan codes found in Match Attax packets to get free digital cards.

STEP 4. Build your digital team and join the fun!

(4) TALKING TACTICS

Change the game with Tactic cards. These super collectable game-changers include injury, referee and agent cards. They can damage an opponent's score, increase your transfer budget, make an opponent swap their player and even boost your cards. You're allowed to use two of them in each match so get them into your squad to take the win!

(5) ATTACKING DEFENDERS, DEFENSIVE ATTACKERS!

Look out for players who are good in attack and defence, mainly all-rounder midfielders and flying full-backs. These guys can spring a shock on an opponent out of nowhere!

SWAP & PLAY TOUR

If you want to find out more about Match Attax, come along to one of our Swap & Play Tour events! You'll be able to swap cards to complete your collection, play games against other collectors and even take part in the Match Attax World Championships!

For more information about dates and events go to topps.com

PARIS SAINT-GERMAIN

Paris Saint-Germain have plenty of heroes and pick up trophies every season. Find out why the French giants are totally fantastique!

TROPHY TALK

After four Ligue 1 titles in a row between 2013 and 2016, Paris Saint-Germain were beaten to the top spot by Monaco in 2017. But they charged back to their seventh championship in 2018, with Edinson Cavani, Kylian Mbappe and Neymar Jr cracking in goals left, right and centre! PSG has won all four domestic titles (Ligue 1, Coupe de France, Coupe de la Ligue and Trophée des Champions) and reached the quarter-finals of the UEFA Champions League.

PLAYER POWER

You'll see more stars in PSG's mega-expensive squad than if you look through a telescope at night! As well as their awesome attacking trio, Thiago Silva, Angel Di Maria and Julian Draxler boss Ligue 1 as their manager Thomas Thuchel drives them on in pursuit of more trophies.

STARS TO WATCH...

KYLIAN MBAPPÉ
STRIKER
Penalty-box predator

THIAGO SILVA
DEFENDER
Cool head & top tackling

MARCO VERRATTI
MIDFIELDER
Ace playmaker

JULIAN DRAXLER
MIDFIELDER
Skilful, with awesome energy

His full name is Neymar da Silva Santos Junior.

Paris Saint-Germain's No.10 joined from Barcelona for a world-record £200 million in 2017!

He hit the net on his debut for Brazil in 2010, aged just 18.

In his first 20 Ligue 1 games, Neymar struck 20 goals.

In 2011 he won the FIFA Puskas Award for a stunning solo goal for Santos against Flamengo.

In January 2018, Neymar scored four goals in an 8–0 Ligue 1 thrashing of Dijon.

At Barcelona he won eight major trophies, including La Liga twice and the UEFA Champions League in 2015.

In 83 Brazil appearances he has already smashed in 53 goals.

CAPTAIN: Thiago Silva **TOP SCORER:** Edinson Cavani (160+) **YOUNG STARS:** Colin Dagba and Tanguy Kouassi

BEST GOALS EVER!

Get ready for spectacular strikes by some of the biggest world stars of all time!

MIKAEL NILSSON
IFK GOTEBORG v PSV Eindhoven
March 17, 1993
- Incredible bending free-kick by the defender
- Nilsson smacked the ball with his right foot
- It sliced through the air and curled past the keeper

You can have this one for free!

Fantastic free-kick power!

LIONEL MESSI
BARCELONA v Getafe
April 18, 2007
- The teenager took the ball in his own half
- Steered and slid past five players
- Drove the ball into the net

CRISTIANO RONALDO
Rayo Vallecano v REAL MADRID
February 26, 2012
- Quick thinking by the Real legend
- Amazing backheel a long way from the goal
- Ronaldo fired Real to the 2012 title

ZINEDINE ZIDANE
Bayer Leverkusen v REAL MADRID
May 15, 2002
- Frenchman fired an epic long-range volley
- He helped Real win the Champions League final
- Incredible technique to strike the ball

RIVALDO
BARCELONA v Valencia
June 17, 2001
- Spectacular overhead kick in 89th minute
- Brazilian scores winner and hat-trick goal
- Secured Barca's spot in the UEFA Champions League

Get me a tissue – I've dribbled everywhere!

JOHAN CRUYFF
AJAX v Helmond Sport
December 5, 1982
- Cruyff tapped his penalty to the side
- Team-mate Olsen rushed into box
- Cruyff took cheeky return to score

ZLATAN IBRAHIMOVIC
PARIS SAINT-GERMAIN v Bastia
October 19, 2013
- Captain Ibrahimovic showed great technique
- Crazy flicked backheel volley
- PSG cruise to 4-0 victory

DIEGO MARADONA
England v ARGENTINA
June 22, 1986
- Stunning solo strike in World Cup quarter-final
- The Napoli star dribbled from his own half
- Beat four challenges and shot past Peter Shilton

LIONEL MESSI
BARCELONA v Real Sociedad
December 12, 2010
- Fantastic dribble and finish in 5-0 win
- Skipped by four players in the box
- Arrowed clever shot back across the goal

MARIO MANDZUKIC
JUVENTUS v Real Madrid, 2017
Epic overhead volley.

MARCO VAN BASTEN
HOLLAND v Soviet Union, 1988
Sweet volley from a tight angle.

GEORGE WEAH
AC MILAN v Verona 1996
Rapid run from his own box.

JAY-JAY OKOCHA
EINTRACHT FRANKFURT v Karlsruher, 1993
Twisting and turning in the area.